Printed in the United States of America

ISBN: 9798716940161

First Printing, 2021

Qualtrics
333 W River Park Dr
Provo, UT 84604

www.qualtrics.com

Exploring Conjoint Analysis

I

CHAPTER 1: Introduction

Walmart founder Sam Walton once said "There is only one boss. The customer. And he can fire everybody in the company from the chairman on down, simply by spending his money somewhere else." Never before has the consumer had more options and consequently, more power. They are at the center of whether any business will ultimately fail or succeed. A company can always find a path to prosperity by winning over customers and then keeping them happy, engaged and excited.
Ok, so you think to yourself 'all I need to do is win over customers and then ensure they keep coming back...well... how do I do that?'.

Shoppers often evaluate alternatives and choose the best available option. In this light, a product or service not optimized for both the consumer and the business, can lead the organization down a disastrous path of committing resources and time to something that won't resonate with the market.

Any product stems from some idea. Sometimes those ideas come from years and years of studying the market and extensive research and analyzing and conceptualizing and then analyzing some more. Other ideas have originated from stubbing a toe. Regardless of how an idea was conceived they typically have to go through rounds of development and improvement until it is ready to go to market. The ideas that actually do go on to achieve success (and that will be a fraction) will eventually become stale in the market and sales will lag. A product needs to be re-invented to keep up with the market. It is most surely an uphill battle.
So, what can the fledgling entrepreneur or seasoned business leader do to increase their chances of releasing and/or improving an appealing product or service? The answer is conjoint analysis. Conjoint analysis identifies the features/functionality you should bank on and the prices you should charge.

Let's say that you think you are really onto something. Your product has resonated well with focus groups but now you have no idea what customers will pay? At the extremes, a too low price point can leave money on the table that is badly needed to fund market expansion and meet new demand... and a too high price may sabotage sales. Conjoint analysis can help pinpoint the price sensitivity of your customers and allow you to lock-in on what the sweet spot will be in pricing your product. Or your service that you offer is slipping in regard to sales and you now realize improvements need to be made. Conjoint analysis can assist with prioritizing what features are most important to the customer base and thus most critical to ensure correct results.

The risks of being wrong in these business problems can severely impact an organization. They can yield stunted growth and misalignment of resources. They can allow the competition to move ahead and control more share of wallet. The risks of being wrong on product decisions can destroy the image of a brand and effectively can be the downfall of a business.

So how are the top organizations improving their odds of releasing wildly successful products and services? How are they approaching the need to reinvent before they become obsolete? How are these companies answering key product questions like "which components of our product are customers focusing in on?', 'what combinations of product features perform better in certain markets?' and 'how much should we be charging for this new service?'.

The answer is Conjoint Analysis.

Conjoint Analysis is a special class of research tools that provides the insight necessary to confidently determine what is important to your customers and what product options optimize your chances of success.

Conjoint analysis can help identify the features and functionality a fledgling entrepreneur can bank on when searching for ways to increase the chances of releasing a star product. Conjoint analysis can add confidence to the seasoned business leader who is re-inventing a product by shedding light on what truly is important to your customer base. And using conjoint analysis can avoid the dilemma of either leaving money on the table by pricing too low or sabotaging sales by pricing too high when determining the pricing sweet spot.

The business problems and questions described in the previous paragraphs come across the desk of business men and women every day. They are critical to answer yet complex in nature. But conjoint analysis is up to the challenge. Conjoint analysis will properly prioritize product development, understand price sensitivity and gain the foresight to leverage competitive advantages. Conjoint analysis yields actionable and accurate data by testing the most realistic decision-making experiences possible via survey results. Additionally, conjoint analysis will model and predict the choice share that can be won when introducing specific product or service combinations within a current or new market.

As we further explain conjoint analysis and its principles, let us consider a situation that may be familiar to many of us.

It's 1pm on a Saturday and Costco is full of shoppers.
(Costco is a big box member-only warehouse store selling a huge variety of items including bulk groceries, electronics and household products)

After working all morning, a few errands are run and lunch is courtesy of the aisle vendors sharing their product samples. Distracted while eating and texting, you almost run head-on into an end-cap of multi-serving dessert packages where Crème Brulee is touted as "The Original Dessert from France." But the "Belgium Dark Chocolate Mousse" trial starts my mouth watering and you rationalize the need for one of the four products on display while reading each label:

"Rians" La Crème Brulee - France, ($6.89 = 6@1.15 ea.)
"Delice" Sea Salt Caramel Dark Chocolate Mousse Parfait - Belgium, ($8.99=6@1.50 ea.)
"Pots and Co." Chocolate Fudge Lava Cake - USA ($11.39 = 4@2.85 each)
"G2G" Organic Almond Coconut Protein Bar - USA ($14.79 = 8@1.85 each)

Assuming this decision process to be all about decadence at less than $15 (rich tasting and something special), and the price is not an important choice criteria, the consumer's choice process may be something like the following:

Protein bar... "Not decadent, not interested."
Fudge Lava Cake from the USA by Pots and Co? "Bad heartburn from last Lava Cake, No."
Crème Brulee from France? "Egg custard, warm and serve, no chocolate. Risky."

"Dilici" package explains the product poorly, but "Dilice" is an image of "delicious", so is "sea salt caramel." The small print links "Belgian" + "dark chocolate" + "mousse." This sounds really good, and anything with caramel is a favorite at home.

Conjoint analysis decomposes the product offering into attributes, features and benefits, as shown below.

Brand name	Rians; Delice; Pots and Co.; G2G
Country of origin	France; Belgium; USA
Dessert type	Custard; Mousse; Cake; Protein bar
Flavor	Vanilla; Caramel/Dark Chocolate; Chocolate Fudge; Almond Coconut
Organic	Organic; Non-Organic
Price per serving	$1.15; $1.50; $1.85; $2.85

The different products on the shelf were all considered but ultimately the reason that put the "Delice" box in your cart is because the _flavor_ component was most influential to you. And specifically, that the flavor was Carmel/Dark Chocolate. This is a situation that each of us go through weekly, if not daily - making trade-off decisions amongst different product offerings in order to maximize our utility. We all evaluate different products (often subconsciously) to gauge what components matter the most (price, flavor, convenience...) and selecting the item that delivers the best experience in that component. The core purpose of conjoint analysis is to provide the data to understand the driving forces in each customer's purchase decision. Then those individual selection behaviors can be aggregated up to understand the market.

Chapter 2: Conjoint Analysis Overview

Conjoint analysis is a market research technique for measuring the preference and importance that respondents (customers) place on the various elements of a product or service. It can play a critical role in understanding the trade-offs that people would make when given different product options and different product configurations. It is typically conducted via online questionnaires where respondents will be shown varying bundles and will be instructed to evaluate and select those bundles based on which they would be most likely to purchase or which is the most appealing to them. The choice selections being made shed light into the features and feature combinations that are showing up more frequently in favorable bundles and of the flipside, which features and feature combinations are more common among the unfavorable bundles. This idea of features either increasing or decreasing the likelihood that a product package is interesting to a buyer and then trying to predictively model the level of likelihood is the essence of conjoint analysis.

Simply, conjoint analysis is a research method for discerning how people choose. It pinpoints the key elements that dictate and control those decisions. These studies yield models for predicting choice behavior.

The output of conjoint analysis allows us to isolate customer's preferences. It delivers the ability to view marketability at a micro level or combine, or 'conjoin', attributes with understanding of bundle comparisons at a macro level. And it does so with both accurate and actionable outcomes.

With conjoint analysis, the increased accuracy is in part attributed to the behind-the-scenes, decompositional approach to understanding people's appeal for features rather than an explicit, stated preference approach of simply asking respondents to rate the various features. Because we are forcing the respondent to make choices across various choice sets, conjoint analysis is also referred to as discrete choice analysis or trade-off analysis. The foundational idea of conjoint analysis is that people cannot accurately and completely express how they view the different features of the product/service in terms of utility. However, studies show that people can do a much better job systematically expressing their value and preference by using these real-world scenarios to tease them out. A *good way* to discover a customer's propensity towards the attributes of a product is to ask them to rate (Likert scale) or rank each of the features and levels. A *better way* would be to *conjoin* the attributes into bundles and ask the respondent to select their favorite option.

In this book we will primarily focus on choice-based conjoint (CBC). Most of the conjoint projects conducted today are a form of CBC and this approach delivers highly insightful findings and is founded upon basic choice exercises that are very familiar to consumers.

There is a lot of jargon and lingo that goes along with conjoint analysis, which can vary depending on factors like: who is running the project, where they learned conjoint analysis, and what platform they use. To avoid confusion, we are going to lay out and explain some key terms and explain what we mean. As this book continues, we will elaborate and define new technical or uncommon terms for the reader.

Attributes can be thought of as the entire set of product/service variables that will be tested as part of the conjoint study. The **attributes** will be the complete structure of factors for the respondent to consider when judging the bundles. The **attributes** will be architected in a nested-hierarchy with multiple variables that can have 2 or more units. **Features** are the groups that encompass the product/service being tested. They would be the variable titles constituted with multiple units (or levels). In our Costco example above, the **features** would be 'Brand name', 'Country of origin', 'Dessert type'... With conjoint analysis, we will be trying to understand the impact and influence of the top-level **features**.
The **levels** are the units found within each of the features. They are the base item of the conjoint study and will be interchanged in the bundles presented to the respondent. In our example above, the **levels** for 'Dessert type' would be 'Custard', 'Mousse', 'Cake' and 'Protein bar'.

A conjoint **project** or **study** is the end-to-end process of taking the initial business questions all the way to the final conclusions. We will often refer to a conjoint 'exercise'. The **exercise** is the experience respondents would go through in evaluating different packages and making selections. It is the choice questions survey-takers answer. A conjoint **task** is synonymous with a conjoint choice question.

Throughout this book we will further explain the details and concepts surrounding conjoint analysis. Topics we will discuss include the history of conjoint analysis, 'why' and 'when' it should be used, the steps for conducting a conjoint project, and how conjoint analysis can be leveraged for positively impacting business use cases.

Our goal in writing this exploration of conjoint analysis is to educate and inform the reader on the ins and outs of this effective research methodology. As business men and women are introduced to, grasp and implement conjoint analysis into their jobs, they will increase their confidence in their decisions and presentations. It will lift their credibility with colleagues as their opinions are strongly backed with foundational data. As organizations adopt the principles of discerning and modeling the trade-offs of customers, they will see an enhanced ability to delight their customers and predict choice behavior. Conjoint analysis can and should be a go-to research approach as market research and math concepts are connected to narrow-in on what really matters to customers and what doesn't.

History of Conjoint Analysis

Earliest evidence of conjoint analysis principles can be traced back to the mid-1960s when mathematical psychologists R. Duncan Luce and John Tukey formulated theories around preference measurement. Around the same time, econometrician Daniel McFadden was developing methods for analyzing discrete choice (he would go on to win a Nobel Prize in Economic Sciences for his work). The work of these scholars caught the eye of Paul E. Green, a marketing professor at the University of Pennsylvania. He applied these ideas in studying how buyers make purchase decisions on multidimensional products and other choice marketing projects. Green is widely accepted as the founder of conjoint analysis.

Much of the early conjoint analysis conducted followed a full-profile card sort approach where physical cards were constructed that described the combination. Then those cards were sorted in order from best to worst. Although being rudimentary, these practices were the beginnings of statistically deducing the preference of variables from a feature set. These methods transitioned to profile cards being rated on a preference scale and using ordinary least squares (OLS) regression analysis to understand the appeal of the attributes being tested.

Conjoint analysis began to pick up more speed in the 1980s with the progression of computer software. In 1985, systems like Adaptive Conjoint Analysis (Sawtooth Software) were made available to run on personal computers. Many developments and improvements came from moving conjoint to computers including: more fluid design and survey setups, streamlined analysis and the use of what-if simulators. Qualtrics founder, Scott Smith, played a role in the growth of the conjoint market in developing software, consulting on groundbreaking projects and launching market research conferences with Paul Green that focused on conjoint analysis, amongst other topics. As we entered the 1990s, discrete choice (choice-based conjoint) principles became prominently associated with conjoint analysis; led by professor Jordan (J.J.) Louviere. Scholars and experts combatted choice-based conjoint approaches initially but eventually conceded the value as new commercial software released by Sawtooth Software focused on discrete choice functionality. Choice-based conjoint was furthered by Greg Allenby with the application of hierarchical Bayes estimation methods for evaluating individual-level utility models with increased accuracy than previous models. Hierarchical Bayesian modeling techniques have greatly expanded within the conjoint space and is the estimation method of choice now for most researchers. Conjoint analysis overall grew tremendously in the 1990s and into 2000s and shows no signs of slowing down. Sawtooth Software has been the industry leader in conjoint analysis software for the past 30 years. They offer an assortment of conjoint methodologies, PhD-level design and analysis techniques and a library of informative white papers. A majority of the researchers and consultants offering conjoint analysis as a service were utilizing Sawtooth to power their studies. Sawtooth has played a monumental role in bringing conjoint analysis to marketing experts everywhere; thus, allowing them to more effectively and efficiently carry out these choice experiments and analysis.

Now several software companies, and hundreds of business consultants, offer conjoint analysis as a headline service to guide and direct their clientele. It is being applied to a variety of different business use cases and is continuing to evolve and spread as new technology and talent recognize the potential of conjoint to infuse fresh and innovative ideas into its community.

The When and Why of Conjoint Analysis

Market research is an immensely broad category that covers any activity or effort used in gaining intelligence on your market; including evaluating opportunities, customers and competition. The wide array of data and insights needing to be gathered leads to a wide array of approaches being utilized. Different problems necessitate different tools. If you are trying to identify groups of customers with similar motivations in your market (in order to better understand how to sell to them), a market segmentation study is probably the tool of choice. If the goal is to evaluate other options your customers have in the market, then analysis on the strengths, weaknesses, opportunities, and threats of the competition would likely be the right market research.

Conjoint analysis is no different. There are specific goals and logic of why and when to run a conjoint study. There are situations that are best served by conjoint. Use conjoint analysis appropriately and it will shed light into the hard-to-reach corners of customer purchasing decisions. These tools can be used to develop predictive capabilities for when customers are faced with an assortment of market offerings. Usage of conjoint analysis tools can help to develop the best price sensitivity models via survey research. Simply, conjoint analysis can be an extraordinary instrument when it is used to answer these particular marketing questions. In this chapter we will focus on the when and why of conjoint analysis.

To recognize when we should use conjoint analysis, it makes sense to re-familiarize ourselves with its purpose. Conjoint analysis is a research technique that highlights what product or service is most important to the customer base and discerns how product characteristics increase preference and value. If conjoint helps in understanding the customer's viewpoint of a product, then it should be incorporated when there are pivotal moments in determining product direction. It should be leveraged in reducing the risk of an approaching product struggling to get off the ground. This intersection of product direction and product opportunity is the laboratory of product development. This is where ideas formulate into actual goods and strategy turns into product structure.

III

Chapter 3: Designing and Developing Product

Product development is the overall process of taking a product from a simple idea all the way to releasing it into the market. It is the overarching period that includes the product brainstorming, strategy, planning, marketing, evaluating, tinkering and commercialization of a new offering. A business is only as good as the product or service they offer and so it is easy to understand the critical work that must go into perfecting what will go to market. Product managers are constantly facing an uphill battle. Not because their viewpoints and strategies aren't sound but rather developing products is difficult work. Everything must be heavily scrutinized and tested with multiple trips back to the drawing board. It's like a massage, if it isn't a little painful, you aren't doing it right.

Despite the time, attention and resources that go into developing new products, the facts are that nearly 90% of them will fail. That is a staggering statistic. What is going wrong? What can be improved? What can explain the simple truth that 9 out of 10 new products fail? There is no simple reason for this failure rate. There are many causes that lead to product frustrations. Maybe the market shifted or a competitive product was released at the same time, or difficulties caused by global politics or a worldwide pandemic. Even trying to list all the reasons why products never get off the ground would be impossible. It is likely that a majority of these companies did not prepare, analyze and verify how to properly market their products. The greatest football teams are sometimes thought to be that way because they have unbelievable gifted players. 'They just have the best Quarterback' or 'Their defensive line is just bigger and stronger than any other team'. But neither the players or the team as a whole would be at the top without months, years and lifetimes of practice, preparation, analyzing opponents, and going back to the drawing board.

So, what can the product team do specifically to practice, prepare and analyze? What can they do to reduce the risk of a product never getting legs? There are tools and practices that product managers and marketers can utilize to greatly improve their understanding of the customers, find what they value and subsequently enhance the chances of market success. These can include:

Concept Testing - Concept Testing is a methodology used in determining how a new business idea (product/service) resonates with a target audience. It focuses on gathering insights around the appeal, positioning, strengths and potential of a new product or service. Concept testing focuses on the basic idea of the product in evaluating how accepting the market will be.

Focus Groups & In-Depth Interviews - Focus groups and in-depth interviews differ from the other practices because it centers on qualitative research rather than quantitative. These research practices aim to engage in conversation with a group or individual. The purpose being to obtain first-hand accounts of what is compelling and interesting about a product and alternatively, what is uninteresting and insignificant about that same product. These approaches are obviously harder to scale but can glean stimulating insights that are personalized and rich.

A/B Testing - A/B testing is a controlled experiment where a product teams can test the success of two different alternatives to ultimately identify a *better* approach. This is commonly conducted on websites and SaaS platforms where the opportunity to create multiple 'products' is plausible. Although this method is often backed with actual financial data, it can be a reactive and a resource-costly approach.

Conjoint Analysis in Product Development

Conjoint analysis is a prime technique for product developers needing to understand feature and functionality focus as they are graduating from an idea to an actual product. Conjoint analysis will allow organizations to understand how different potential bundles will stack up to each other, as well as to the competition, before they ship a product. And they can do so when there is still time to shape it in a way that highlights the elements most important to the purchaser. Because after all, a product developer's

15

core job is to create offerings that the market will buy. To properly fulfill this responsibility, conjoint analysis should be used as it is the premiere methodology for discerning what product configuration maximizes the chances of a purchase.

Conjoint analysis can be a key instrument at multiple points of the product development life-cycle. Maturing a product can be grouped into a four-stage act:

1. **Generating the idea**: Generating a product idea is where it all begins. Ideas can germinate in different environments and settings. However, the ideas that usually contain the most potential are the ones that specifically solve customer pain points.

2. **Evaluating the idea**: Evaluating the product idea is not a short or painless task. It is carried out during collaborative brainstorm sessions, discussions, debates in conjunction with strong analysis. The evaluation of that product idea must be thorough and complete because you are often betting the business on it.

3. **Researching and developing**: Once the product idea has passed the evaluation stage and stakeholders are confident in viability, more analysis, research and planning should then be conducted to maximize the development and engineering cycles. Not all features and functionality are perceived equal by customers and not all are fiscally equal in terms of their engineering costs to the business. Because of this, development cycles should be governed by consumer preference and fiscal projections. The research and development period should consist of development forums, Kanban boards and sprint cycles. But it should also be fueled and reinforced with what the customer is sharing about their purchase decisions via product experience research.

4. **Promoting and marketing**: Once the product is shaped and nearing release, product marketers must step in to understand the product options most compelling to the buyer. First, they need to have a certainty of who the buyer is and what pain points the product is solving. They must anticipate what the market will navigate towards within the product feature set and what they should subsequently be highlighting. This is the stage where the go-to-market strategy must be determined in order to empower and direct the sales motion.

No matter the stage of product development, data and consumer insights need to be the compelling force that should direct product and engineering strategy. Conjoint analysis can provide invaluable discernment in guiding how to shape and think about a potential product or service. It can contribute to the early steering and avoid expensive recycling of engineering effort and unnecessary delays. Think about it, having to postpone the release of a new product by 6 months because you found out late that missing functionality is a deal-breaker, can result in being second (or worse) to market and can cause you to lose out on the opportunity to write your own story. Conjoint can be used as the pathway pivots during the development course and as there are shifts with internal resources and external markets.

Conjoint can also be a contributor to the promotion and marketing phase of product development. Consider this scenario, you have a new product you are shipping that contains approximately 40 unique features. All are important and removing one of the features equates to the product missing the mark and no longer being world-class. If the statistics about the percentage of products that fail tells us anything, it is that we need to do all we can to ensure we *don't* miss the mark. So, on that note, we know that functionality can't be removed. However, trying to highlight all 40 features through marketing and advertising would be overwhelming and inefficient because some attributes don't mean much to customers. That is where conjoint analysis can come in (as well as MaxDiff Analysis - a cousin to Conjoint). Conjoint can identify the focus of buyers when deciding what to purchase. Those features that rise to the top of the importance meter within the conjoint study should be the ones that are brought to the forefront of the marketing and promoting efforts.

At any point in developing products, data should be at the forefront of your decision making. Too often companies have left product strategy up to HIPPO (highest paid person's opinion) rather than collecting insights from the only opinion that really matters; the buyer's opinion. Just trusting the assumptions of the well-experienced or even worse, just guessing, can be costly and reckless.

There are times in the lifetime of a product that changes must be made and improvements implemented. It might be because the product has capped out and is no longer resonating with the target audience. It might be that the buyer's needs have shifted and are no longer being solved by your product's functionality. Or it might be that the competition has surpassed you and a product revolution is needed to recapture market share. Regardless of the reason why, it is very common that a product must reinvent itself.

There was a sign that hung in our high school weight room:

> 'When you aren't improving, your opponent is and when you meet, they will win'.

Although this was a simple tactic our coach used to try and inspire lazy teenagers, there is a lot of truth here. Truth that absolutely applies to business and to product management and development. A stale product is usually prime ground for decreased growth and leads to losing customers to the competition. Improving a product and increasing its functionality to address more of the customer's headaches should continually be on the product owner's agenda.

Conjoint analysis can be a barometer in assessing what can be added or changed to our offering to make it better. Conjoint can answer questions like:

- What is the most impactful feature we are considering?
- What are the biggest levers a business can pull improve a product?
- Can we increase the price if we add this set of features?

Conjoint analysis is an incredible tool in answering the key product facelift questions. A distinct advantage available to researchers is to test new product alterations versus the existing baseline product to identify where the greatest preference lift can take place. This methodology can result in elevated confidence in what product upgrades should take place and how the market will respond to them.

Ultimately, conjoint analysis is a premiere technique in the research to fuel developing products. The strengths of conjoint are well suited to tackle the common questions of building products.

At the end of the day, the customer will be buying your offering because they value it more than other options. They will be making discrete decisions with their dollars. And considering that the goal of any product development is to create a more appealing output that brings in more of those decision dollars - it makes sense an approach that runs respondents through realistic choice sets is the superior method for uncovering what matters most to your customers. Trade-off decisions are something we do on a daily basis whether we recognize it or not. On occasion my wife is desperate enough to send me to the grocery store to pick up something like laundry detergent because we have run out (I usually come back with the wrong thing). In those situations, I have to go and make trade-off decisions between the different options available on the shelves. In this situation my decision could be based on the brand (no), the scent (not really), maybe the price (always impacts) or the size (bingo!) The bigger it is, the longer it will be before I have to go back and do it all over again. Conjoint yields actionable and accurate data to select preferred trade-offs to identify the features consumers are zeroing in on (like the detergent size in my case) that really makes the difference.

What are the primary questions that Conjoint Analysis answers

Research is the collecting of information about a particular subject with the goal of answering some question(s). In business, different types of research is conducted because there are many questions to answer; all with the purpose of providing insights and explanations to key business queries. These are the insights and explanations that will foster the businesses' strategy and targets. Jim Barksdale, the former CEO of Netscape, said "If we have data, let's look at data. If all we have are our opinions, let's go with mine." The best companies fuel their decisions with data and research. They utilize studies focused on gathering facts rather than feelings. This data comes in all different shapes and sizes and the methods of collecting that data depends on the questions being asked.

There are key business research objectives that conjoint targets. Conjoint analysis has core questions it specializes in answering. Questions that no other methodology can answer. Those questions can be:

- What feature or functionality of a product is most important and influential in measuring the market's preference and appeal?
- What is a customer's focus when making their purchase decisions?
- What has the greatest impact on whether they will purchase or not?
- What role does price play in decision making and what are the pricing sweet spots?

- How sensitive will customers be to shifts in pricing?
- What is the monetary or relative value to the market of each of the features we are thinking about including?
- How much more would they be willing to pay for a premium feature?
- What trade-offs will our customers be likely to make?
- If we know we need to increase price, what features/functionality can we add to our offering to not lose appeal and market share?
- What does market share look like for different potential product bundles we are looking at?
- How does the shifting and changing of our bundle configuration affect market share?
- How do the product bundles we are considering compare to the competition?
- What can we do to best compete against what is currently on the market?
- If we are looking to make changes to our existing product, what are the best improvements we can make?
- What will resonate best with our existing customers?
- What is the optimal product that we can offer to increase the number of buyers? To maximize our revenue? To maximize our profits?

In a later chapter, we provide examples and further details that educate the reader on exactly how to respond to these questions when using conjoint analysis.

As you can see, conjoint analysis is diverse and dynamic with respect to the critical business questions needing clarity. And these are just the product related inquiries it answers. The length and relevancy of this list is a primary reason why those familiar with conjoint analysis are so fond of them. They provide vision into a wide array of business objectives and provide crucial confidence to researchers and organizations.

IV

Chapter 4: How Conjoint Analysis is conducted

Experiments are procedures where a series of steps are carried out to support or validate a hypothesis. The following of the designated steps within any experiment require focus and allegiance to ensure the result obtained at the outcome of the study is sound and factual. The steps are critical in leading us to a reputable result.

Any form of market or product research is analogous with experimental research where there is a sequence to the methodology. With survey research, the general checkboxes are: determine the objectives, design the study, program the survey, collect responses, analyze the results and report on the findings. These steps give credence to the beginning, middle and end of the project so that researchers don't reach the conclusion of the study with faulty data and/or findings.

This definitely rings true for conjoint analysis. In fact, it might be even more imperative to pursue the proper steps because of the mathematical nature of the backend analysis. The phrase 'garbage in, garbage out' is absolutely true with conjoint. Mishaps like presenting respondents with an insufficient set of conjoint bundles can result in an inability to achieve any sort of trustworthy conclusions. So, it is paramount that the steps are understood and checked off when a conjoint analysis is being carried out.

The steps for running a conjoint analysis are:
1. Determine the attributes to be tested within the conjoint analysis
2. Generate the experimental design
3. Program the survey that hosts the conjoint tasks
4. Collect responses
5. Analyze the conjoint results
6. Report the findings

Each of these build upon the previous action in working toward the end goal of understanding the favorable trade-offs and preferences of the customer base. When the conditions and steps are adhered to, researchers can be confident in data being derived. When they are neglected, the results are likely disastrous.

Determine the attributes to be testing in the conjoint analysis
The start of any research is consumed by the asking of questions. 'What do we want to find out?', 'Who are we targeting?', 'What will we do with the results?' ... These are all applicable to conjoint but the first primary questions is typically 'what are we wanting to test?'. See, once we know what we are going to test, the rest of the study can take its shape. The 'what' will formulate the building blocks of our research. However, locking down the variables, attributes or characteristics we are going to test is not a simple or trivial step. Sometimes it can be more of an art as it is a science. Researchers can begin formulating the attribute list by reviewing market offerings, internal brainstorming and primal survey research to narrow down broader lists. This can often be the longest process (in terms of time) within a conjoint study as stakeholders discuss the specifics of what should be included. There is often back and forths on what gets included, the wording and how it all should be structured.

The framework of the variables we are looking to incorporate in a conjoint study is that of features and levels. The features are the primary categories or groups of the variables with each one of those consisting of a set of levels or units. Examples usually help for comprehension:

Features	Levels
Main dish	Chicken, Steak, Seafood
Side dish	Fries, Salad, Soup
Drink	Water, Soda
Price	$10, $15, $20, $25

Figure 4.1: Example of Conjoint study to test dinner packages

There is a tricky balance of deciding which features and levels will be incorporated in the study because if you don't test a variable, you obviously will get zero vision into its preference. While testing too many features and levels can lead to respondent fatigue, inconsistent responses and worthless data. Respondent fatigue is widely considered the biggest enemy of conjoint analysis as the quality of the model depends upon consistent and accurate response selections. There is not a one-size-fits-all approach in the number of variables to be tested. Although different types of conjoint can facilitate more or less variables, traditionally we would recommend to include around 2-8 features with 2-7 levels per feature. Keep in mind that the more features and levels you include, the more difficult the exercise will be for respondents as the number of questions likely increase as well as the amount of information for them to process. Simply put, the more features and levels tested, the more overwhelming the conjoint will be for survey-takers. It can be a tug-a-war between whether or not to include a product attribute. Groups should carefully consider what should be inserted into the conjoint and should be disciplined in their admittance.

Regardless of the number of attributes you bring to the conjoint, it is essential that they are clear and concise. If the respondents can't grasp the bundles they are reviewing, the data will mean nothing. The text used for both the features and their levels should describe them plainly but acutely. The study creator should consider and even focus on the survey-taker and their context of the product/offering being examined. Ask yourself 'will someone outside our walls understand the bundles being presented'? Ensuring that the survey and specifically the conjoint tasks are unmistakable will return enriching results. Though on the flipside lengthy text can clutter the page and make the choice tasks daunting and overwhelming. A fantastic enhancement can be using images when finding the right words to define an attribute seems challenging. 'A picture is worth a thousand words' can absolutely ring true in conjoint analysis.

While the team is determining the product factors to investigate, it is important to be looking out for combinations that just don't make sense to combine. What we are _not_ talking about is two levels that likely would never be conjoined but rather two levels that would be confusing and impossible to pair in real-life. These are typically referred to as exclusions or prohibited pairs. These should only be called out when presenting such a combo would disorient the respondent. In the design section to follow we will talk about why we want to avoid overdoing it with prohibited pairs but these should be thought out and identified at the onset of the project.

The Experimental Design

The nature of most conjoint analysis projects is that not all of the possible combinations can be displayed to a respondent. Every combination, or the full factorial, can easily reach into the hundreds or thousands. Obviously, we could never show each respondent every possible bundle. But then the question is posed of how do we obtain insights on the favorability of the different mixtures?

Incorporating statistical experimental designs principles into the combinations that will be presented is essential to the quality of the data collected. Similar to other experimental approaches, strategic and scientific ideas are leveraged in deciphering how to get a preference read on the entire combination space while still only showing a subset and avoiding respondent fatigue. **The core idea behind experimental designs in conjoint is simply how do we maximize the number of data points and coverage of the potential packages while minimizing the number of profiles we expose to each respondent.**

There are several approaches in determining the cards that will be presented to the respondent. In the past when computers were not as accessible and as powerful as they are now, predefined design tables were generated and referenced by researchers. You would identify the number of features and levels (often a 3x3 or a 4x4) and go find the corresponding design table and incorporate that into your survey. These however reduced the amount of flexibility most researchers wanted in defining the feature attribute space.

Now, most choice based conjoint and rating based conjoint designs incapsulate fractional factorial card sets that will be presented to respondents. Fractional factorial means that we will show a fraction of the full factorial or a subset of the possible combinations. There are several key ingredients in determining what subset of profiles will be displayed within the questionnaire. Card sets should have relative balance across each level. This means that within a feature, each level should be included in a similar number of bundles. There shouldn't be one level that is shown in six bundles while another level is only included once. As with any survey research, randomization techniques improve the validity of responses and control psychology order bias. Frequently, the research will generate a wide variety of package subsets to be presented in the questions. These are called versions or blocks. Conjoint designs are best suited when there are a lot of versions that all incorporate their own unique subset of bundles. Jordan Louviere and

Sawtooth Software Founders both agree that the more versions that are a part of the overall design, the better. A respondent would be assigned to one of those versions which would dictate packages that would be presented.

Other principles that are often discussed with conjoint designs are orthogonality and d-efficiency. There are debates and back-and-forths on the necessity and importance of integrating these concepts into the experimental design for conjoint studies.

The inputs at the base of generating designs for choice-based conjoint is the number of questions or tasks that will be presented to the respondent as well as the number of choices or alternatives there will be per question. The traditional CBC approach typically calls for two choices where the respondent chooses between option A and option B. That being said, it is definitely appropriate to show three or more bundles per question for the respondent to evaluate. The important query that needs to be thought through is if more alternatives will create an overwhelming and overly complex experience for the respondent. It is likely that evaluating more than two bundles for preference can be a daunting task. Additionally, if a 'none of these' option is to be included in the study, screen space might lend to a better experience with just two choices and the none choice. The number of questions that will comprise the conjoint portion of the survey should be calculated based on the number of choices per task as well as the size of the conjoint attributes being tested. The general formula for determining the number of cards that should be displayed is:

Number of Cards = Total # of Levels - # of Feature + 1

The total # of levels is found by adding the number of levels across all of the features. Based upon the total number of cards and the number of choices per question, it is easy to reverse engineer the number of questions that will be necessary.

Where the design can take on the form of art more than science is when determining if the survey needs to be shortened by reducing the number of questions and increasing the number of bundles per question. Or determining if that hurts the data quality. The best approach for resolving the balance between questions and alternatives per question is to simply test. Create the survey and click through it. Distribute it to colleagues and get their opinion on the weight of the question versus the length of the survey. That will be the best indication on if you should reduce the number of alternatives within each question or extend the number of conjoint questions included.

Other theories that should be considered when planning the experimental design are: prohibited pairs, conditional pricing and alternative specific designs. Prohibited pairs, mentioned in the *Determining Attributes* step, should be done cautiously as they normally decrease the efficiency of the design and reduce the accuracy of the results. A useful trick in regard to these exclusions is to collapse the two attributes involved in the prohibition into a one single attribute that represents the combination. Conditional pricing is beneficial to conjoint designs when there is a feature that heavily impacts the price shown with the rest of the bundle. An example of this would be if we were testing a dinner offering and we had a feature such as the main dish. It would be difficult to try and price Prime Rib, BBQ Chicken or a Club Sandwich all with the same pricing levels. Conditional pricing would follow a strategy of a low, medium and high price for each main dish option as seen below :

	Low	Medium	High
Prime Rib	$35	$45	$55
BBQ Chicken	$10	$15	$20
Club Sandwich	$7	$12	$15

Figure 4.2

Alternative specific designs are a specialized type of experimental designs used when certain variables don't make sense to combine with other variables. The typical use case is when you have a primary variable that dictates what can and can't be paired with it. An example (Figure 4.3) of this would be viewing NBA basketball games. The primary variable would be how you view the game: Buy season tickets to attend the game, Purchase NBA League Pass, Go to an eating establishment. All of these options are paired with a price but other features like 'Transportation time to the game' only applies to buying season tickets. Alternative specific designs can be very helpful when there are attributes that don't commonly share inclusiveness but it is important to keep in mind that considerations need to be taken in regard to the modeling, analysis and simulations of the project.

Season Tickets	Buy League Pass	Eating Establishment
Price: $955 $1395 $1995	Price: $25 $35 $45	Price: Free
		Reserved Spot: Yes No
Transportation Time: 20min 40min 60min		

Figure 4.3

Survey Programming

Conjoint analysis is made possible by the responses collected through surveys. The survey is the touchpoint wherein the respondents are presented the design and trade-off selections are made. When a conjoint study is conducted, it is usually the focus of the survey but not always the entirety of it. It is critical though that the conjoint exercise within the survey is concise and well structured. The data and insights will only be as accurate as the packages are clear.

The questionnaire commonly includes screener questions (to ensure the right type of respondent is providing feedback), introduction and educational resources for the respondent as well as demographic questions. There are no hardened rules on how many other questions can be added to a conjoint study or where in the survey flow the conjoint should fall. It should be noted that any question being asked of the respondents outside of the conjoint takes up time and focus that could otherwise be given to the conjoint exercise. Survey length should be considered as the study is being designed and built out. Fatiguing a respondent is a surefire way of harming the caliber of the study. Surveys that take more than 10-15 minutes are more susceptible to fatigue and data quality issues

The data fielded from a conjoint study is only relative and accurate if the respondent can realistically put themselves in the actual purchasing setting. Assuring that the respondent is fully aware and informed on the packages they will be reviewing and selecting amongst is critical to the success of conjoint analysis. Many studies are testing concepts that are well known and relatable by the general public. However, if that is not the case with your project, time should be devoted in advance of the conjoint to properly educate the respondent through descriptions and/or videos. The more clear and imaginable a package is to the survey-taking, the more true the utilities will be. In addition to the text and descriptions being simple and straightforward, the layout of the cards should also lend to understanding and clarity. This allows the respondent to make comparisons and answer definitively.

Collecting Responses

Critical to the success and accuracy of the conjoint results is the number of responses needed as well as the relevance of the individuals taking the survey. A proper equation for determining the number of responses is:

# of respondents = (500*c)/(t*a)

c=# of levels in the feature with the most levels
t=number of tasks or questions
a=number of alternatives or choices per question

A more general approach for discrete choice conjoint would be to aim for 300 responses for smaller projects and 500 responses for larger projects in terms of number of conjoint attributes.

It is important that the individuals taking the conjoint exercise are reflective of those that would be at play to purchase, order or opt for your product or service. Frequently, researchers will define screeners at the beginning of the questionnaire to ensure only pertinent opinions are gathered. Alternatively, groups will often have lists of current or prospective customers that they can distribute surveys to.

Analyzing Conjoint Results

Analyzing conjoint projects is where data turns into actual models and predictions. It is where respondent selections are transformed into preferences. The outcome of the analysis will be an understanding of what is valuable to customers and what is not and will paint the picture of how product features should be bundled.

The core of the analysis is the statistical modeling that estimates the utility that respondents assign to each level. This statistical modeling is where conjoint analysis gets its 'complex' reputation but this is also what enables conjoint to be a world-class research technique. The typical method for analyzing conjoint data is a multinomial logit model. MNL is a regression technique used for multidimensional variable structures to ultimately yield prediction likelihoods of attributes and entire packages being selected from a lineup.

The output of the conjoint modeling will be utility coefficients that represent the value or preference that the respondent base has for the distinct levels of each feature. For designs and analysis methods that allow for individual-level calculations of utility scores, we can derive preference models for every single respondent. This can be advantageous for a number of reasons including segmentation of various data cuts, latent class analysis and simulations. The primary approach taken to yield individual-based utility models is hierarchical Bayesian (further referred to as 'HB') estimation. This is a technique that uses Bayesian principles to probabilistically derive the relative value of each variable causing a 'purchase' or 'selection'.

HB is an iterative process that is 'hierarchical' because it encompasses two levels; an upper level model that pinpoints the overall population's parameters through a normal distribution and a lower level model that produces individual specific preferences. These two work together until the analysis converges on the coefficients that represent the value of each attribute. The HB technique borrows information from other responses to gain more stable individual-level results. It is very robust and allows us to get really good reads into the preferences even while presenting less tasks to the respondent.

Reporting the Findings
With the derived utility coefficients at the base of the analysis, outputs and deliverables can be prepared to showcase the findings of the study. They will be the building blocks of all of the summary metrics and simulations. The core summary metrics that typically accompany conjoint analysis are:

Feature importance: The amount of influence and impact that a feature has in decision-making amongst product configurations. The greater the feature importance, the more weight and control it has in what makes a favorable product. Feature importance is calculated by taking the distance between the best and worst level within that feature. The bigger the distance, the more important the feature. A simple way to think about feature importance is that if the levels of that feature have a big impact on whether or not a package is selected or not, then that is a really important feature.

Average Utility Scores: The average utility score of each level across all respondents. These are ordinal in nature and will show the relative preference between levels. The average utilities can give some directional understanding but should not be a standalone metric to summarize the conjoint analysis.

First Choice Preference Scores: The first choice preference scores indicate the percentage of respondents that had their highest utility for each of the different levels. Within each respondent's utility coefficients they will have a top or most preferred level within each feature.

Preference Share: The preference share is the measurement of the probability that a level would be chosen over another with all else feature components held constant. It is a product of the utilities being calculated using a Multinomial Logistic model and is derived by taking the log-likelihood ('EXP' function in Excel) the level utility and dividing that by the sum of all of the log-likelihoods of levels within the feature.

Willingness to Pay: The amount of money a customer is willing to pay for a particular attribute of a product in comparison to another attribute. Typically, we recommend that a base case or current case level is defined and then we can determine how much more or less they are willing to pay in comparison to the base level. Each level can have a willingness to pay compared to the base case. This can only be used when price or cost is a feature in the conjoint analysis. It is calculated by finding the amount of utility difference between the tested price points and then applying that dollar per utility ratio to the other levels and their utility scores. We usually like to calculate the willingness to pay on the respondent level and then aggregate and summarize.

Optimal packages: This is the optimal package in regard to maximizing customer preference and appeal. This might not always be the exact approach an organization would want to move toward, as the cost of implementation may be prohibitive, but it can guide directionally. Often the overarching goal of conjoint is to understand how bundles/packages compare to each other. Organizations need to understand the share of preference between different combinations and identify market share against competing offers. They need to see whether preference increases and decreases as changes are made to the bundles. Because of this, often the primary tool that stakeholders want to leverage is a simulator.

A simulator is an interactive tool that facilitates the testing and balancing of preference amongst plausible product configurations. The simulator typically includes a series of dropdowns that allows for creation of packages from the attributes that were tested within the study. At the core, conjoint analysis is a technique for recognizing the trade-offs that customers would make when presented with different choices. The preference simulator embodies this mission by reporting the estimated trade-offs that customers would make when presented with two or more options.

In addition to the obvious trade-off analysis, there are a variety of use cases that can be extremely valuable in pulling insights from conjoint results. The most prevalent practices using the simulator are: running competitive landscape analysis, improvement from a product base case and the relative value of product attributes.

Competitive landscape analysis with a simulator
Healthy businesses will frequently be looking over their shoulder to research how the competition compares. Conjoint analysis is a great tool to uncover how a potential product configurations would compare versus competing options on the market. This is contingent however on the attributes of the competing products being included in the studies features and levels. Within the simulator, the competitor's product attributes can be laid out and then with the remaining option/package you can define different bundles to preview how they would stack up to the existing market.

Improving an existing product with a simulator

Oftentimes in business, products need to go through revamps and improvements to stay ahead of competitors and remain relevant and innovative. This requires progressive adjustments. A conjoint study is a fantastic methodology for understanding where companies can make the most compelling changes to excite new prospects and retain their current users. With data in hand, a simulator can be utilized to capture the what-ifs of making changes to the product attributes. *'Option 1'* within the simulator would be laid out to be the current product and with *'Option 2'*, the controller would start with the same current product line and then make iterative changes to the available attributes to distinguish where the biggest gains are available.

Gauging the relative value of product attributes with a simulator
Any product is at its core, a combination of multiple features. It is a sum of its parts. Grasping the preference of those parts is an essential piece of conjoint analysis. Expanding upon 'preference', it makes sense to try and further quantify the value of each level. If price was included within the attribute set, the simulator can be an outstanding tool for inferring that value. The process would be to mirror the same product configuration in *'Option 1'* and *'Option 2'*. By changing a single level or group of levels, you will find the preference share no longer equal. With the other option, move the price level to find where the two packages now are equal again. The difference in price between *'Option 1'* and *'Option 2'* can be interpreted as the relative value of that level or group of levels.

Now that we better understand the steps of how conjoint analysis is conducted, we can better grasp how key business questions are answered. Earlier, we laid out those core business objectives that conjoint sheds light on but how and why does conjoint fulfill these. Let us go through each one to more fully understand.

V

Chapter 5: Types of Conjoint Analysis

Conjoint analysis is the methodology category for uncovering consumer preferences by forcing them to make trade-offs. The exact presentation of those trade-offs for the collecting of data can vary though. There are different types of conjoint analysis that specialize for different use cases and purchase decision-making. Some of these conjoint variations are more prevalent and flexible than others but all have their time and place for providing important insights into choice modeling. In the next section we will further explain each of the different methods and describe the scenarios that they are best suited for.

Choice-Based Conjoint

Choice-based conjoint (CBC) is the most common form of conjoint analysis and what those who have had exposure with conjoint will most likely be familiar with. CBC is also frequently called discrete choice conjoint as the respondent is presented with multiple bundles and asked to select (a discrete choice) the one they prefer most or would be most likely to purchase. Typically in CBC, there are 2 or 3 bundles that are displayed for the respondent to choose between. The construction of those bundles and their configurations are based on the experimental design that is being incorporated. With this approach, the design is generated ahead of the survey launch with the idea being that we want to ensure that across the respondents and their selections, we will have sufficient data to model preferences. The respondent data is modeled using some form of correlation analysis to identify what levels/features give the best indication if a package would or would not be selected.

Frequently with CBC, a 'none of these' option is included to allow the respondent to flag if none of the bundles are compelling enough. This allows survey-takers to indicate an outside good is better than those presented. The 'outside good' could be that they would buy another product if those presented were what your company was offering. Or it could be that they would not purchase anything if the options displayed were the only packages available to them. Installing the none option within the conjoint exercise is best suited when the project's objective is to focus on market adoption projections. When the goal is centered on research and development and in maximizing the contents included in a bundle, then the none option should not be used. On top of the none selection, CBC can also be coupled with a *dual choice* method where the initial choice task does not include a 'none' option but where it is immediately followed by a question where the respondent is asked if they would actually purchase the bundle they selected above. This can force the survey-taker to give meaningful feedback on the best presented package while also elaborating on if it is good enough to lead them to spending their money.

The best practices for a CBC project is two to eight features with each of those features having between two and seven levels. That will yield two to twelve conjoint questions with each question having between two and four choices or alternatives. The sweet spot for a conjoint exercise would be 4 to 8 questions.

A concentration within CBC that can be used is incorporating **alternative specific** designs. These designs include some of the product attributes having their own unique sets of levels. A frequent use case of alternative specific designs is around price where the cost included with the different packages is conditional upon a variable like brand.

Adaptive Choice-Based Conjoint
Adaptive choice-based conjoint (ACBC) is an advancement from regular CBC. The discrete choice exercise where respondents selected their preference bundle is still at the core of the adaptive approach but with additional design considerations to optimize the respondent experience. The survey experience for the respondent is similar to CBC but as the survey continues, the bundles become more relevant to respondents with the use of submitted data. The concept is similar to the experience of a Pandora music application where the songs and artists the user will hear going forward are adapted to them based on the 'thumbs-up' and 'thumbs-down' they have submitted to the songs they have already listened to.

Adaptive choice-based conjoint is an evolution on top of the CBC framework. Although the specifics of the adaptation of packages for selection can vary, the most well-known approach was pioneered by Sawtooth and includes the respondent going through a Build-Your-Own section, a Concept Screener section, a Choice Task section (very similar to a standard CBC), and finishes with a Concept Tournament section. Although a survey response takes longer through this method, studies show that respondents are presented more interesting and compelling questions and thus have a more engaging experience.

Others prefer a more efficient adaptive conjoint exercise that uses the simplicity of choice tasks that also leverages adaptation. An alternative approach is to run the respondent through an initial ranking exercise where the respondent arranges the high-level features in terms of importance and the impact they have on their decision-making. The rank-order exercise is then passed through to a design algorithm that pulls the levels from those top features. The respondent is shown a partial feature profile that is based upon their stated importance ranking. This path tailors the options to showcase more compelling and simpler bundles for the respondent to select from. This reduces the number of question tasks that a respondent would be presented. It is important that this approach is used on concepts that the survey taker has some familiarity with and understands the value that the different features offer. This style is favorable when a large attribute set is to be tested as it reduces the number of cards the subject evaluates and thus reduces the risk of respondent fatigue.

It would be recommended that a hierarchical Bayesian approach is used in estimating the preferences of an adaptive conjoint because there will be missing parameters amongst the different individuals and there will be the need to recover those preferences by borrowing information from the population. This is exactly what HB modeling facilitates.

Full-Profile Conjoint
Full-profile conjoint analysis was used heavily at the onset of conjoint analysis and is how most of the early conjoint projects were conducted. The idea is that a respondent is shown all of the variations of the concept and typically asked to rate it on a Likert scale. Researchers often tried to keep these projects uncomplicated by including a small set of attributes and presenting the full factorial to each respondent to rate.

This was the primary method for collecting data thirty years ago but as design approaches and technology have improved, the popularity of this methodology has dropped.

Self-Explicated Conjoint
Self-explicated conjoint analysis is a hybrid approach where the respondent isn't presented bundles or packages. Rather, they are asked to rate the levels and the features independently. The evaluation process is simple and always takes the respondent through just three screens. First, they select their best and worst level within each feature. Second, they rate the remaining levels on a 0 to 10 scale, using the pre-selected 'best' and 'worst' levels as anchor points. Lastly, the respondent is asked to allocate 100 points amongst the top-level attributes to indicate feature importance.

The output of self-explicated conjoint analysis would be very similar to any other type where you would have respondent level utility scores that could be used for comparisons and simulations. It is a nice technique for gathering initial data on the preferences of a customer-base. It is important to note that this method completely falls short when variables like price are included as it doesn't force the respondent to make trade-offs between bundles. For this reason, most researchers are hesitant to base findings and projections solely on the outcomes of self-explicated conjoint analysis.

Menu-Based Conjoint
Menu-based conjoint analysis (or MBC) is a form of conjoint analysis where respondents are presented the attributes/levels being included in the study and are asked to build their own packages based on their preferences. This replaces the exercise of them being shown bundled choice tasks to make discrete choices between. They select their optimal attributes from a menu, thus the name menu-based conjoint.

With MBC studies, price is typically used as a constraint and is updated on the total package cost as options are included and removed from their self-made bundle. In comparison, it can be a more interactive experience where the respondent feels more in control rather than just responding to bundles already arranged. It can be especially engaging when the real-world purchase experience resembles an event of choosing from a menu. The downside of this approach is that the coverage of the model is typically not as exhaustive as a design-based conjoint methodology. We would get a sense of the most important levels but lose some ability to simulate the trade-offs between the lesser preferred attributes. The analysis of MBC is typically conducted with counts analysis as well as modeling with Bayesian estimation techniques.

Perceptual Choice Conjoint
Perceptual choice conjoint analysis is typically an extension to a standard CBC exercise. This approach focuses on adding context to the 'why' they prefer a bundle. Researchers can often want to know not only what trade-off a customer would make between bundles but also why they would choose one bundle over another.

This is done by adding a question to the bottom of each discrete choice task that uses a multi-select question to pinpoint which perceptual items are tied to each bundle. The 'reason why' statements selected are used in estimating the likelihood that the respective conjoint levels would contribute to a product bundle being agreeable with the different perceptions.

Volumetric Conjoint
The idea behind Volumetric conjoint is to add a quantity aspect to the equation. Oftentimes in the real-world (especially with grocery-type goods) it is not just a matter of selecting product 1 over product 2 but rather how much of each product the customer would purchase.

The design portion of a Volumetric conjoint is very similar to that of a choice-based project where bundles are strategically presented to ensure balance and coverage in the explanatory matrix. The key differentiation between Volumetric and other forms of conjoint analysis is in the actual responses given by the respondent. Rather than a discrete selection, the survey-taker provides the amount of units they would purchase.

In the modeling of Volumetric Conjoint projects, the number of units are used as the response variable when estimating the prowess and preference of the individual levels that make up the product concepts. This can yield better predictions of quantity and identify product bundles that would maximize profits.

VI

Chapter 6: How Conjoint Analysis Answers Key Business Questions

In an earlier chapter, we listed business questions that conjoint analysis provides key insights towards. Answering these questions are critical for organizations looking to progress their business. The sheer length of the list is a fundamental reason why those familiar with conjoint analysis return to the well and frequently leverage it. The observations below are not meant to be exhaustive but should assist the reader in further grasping the outcomes derived from running conjoint analysis.

- What feature or functionality of a product is most important and influential in measuring their preference and appeal?

   The output of conjoint analysis yields individual utility coefficients. These represent the relative preference that each respondent has for the tested variables. As they are aggregated to calculate a total bundle utility, we can estimate the likelihood that a respondent would select/purchase that bundle versus a lineup of other bundles. In this way, we can estimate the influence and preference that each distinct level has on each individual as well as the total population. We can measure the influence and impact of the categories or features by evaluating the shift in likelihood to purchase that happens as we move from the least preferred level to the most preferred level. If going from the worst to the best level and vice versa causes a large shift in the overall likability, then this feature would have a large feature importance score.

   To help further communicate this response, we can walk through an example. Let's say we are running a conjoint project on a printer. We have 8 features but the two we will focus on are *'price' and 'size of interface screen'. When we go from the most preferred price ($399) to the least preferred ($999) while keeping all other attributes constant, the preference share drops 54%. For the size of the interface screen the worst level is 4 inches and the best is 8 inches. When we move from 8" to 4" the share declines just 9%. Because of this, we would say that price is a lot more influential or important to customers than the size of the interface screen.*

- What are customers focused on when making their purchase decision - what has the greatest impact on whether they will purchase or not?

It is one thing to grasp what makes a product more appealing and preferred. It is a lot more valuable to know what makes a product appealing enough to lead customers to actually purchase. Conjoint analysis can do both. Similar to the approach explained above, conjoint can identify what attributes are impacting selections for better or worse. We can also understand the affinity to purchase different bundles by adding a 'none' option or by utilizing a dual-choice question where immediately after the choice selection we ask if they would actually purchase the package they selected. What this provides the model is a read into what contributes to a package positively enough to lead a customer to want to buy it. In our analysis, if the total bundle utility of a package is greater than the utility of some 'outside good' (choosing not to purchase) then we can assume that they would purchase.

41

	Change in Preference Share	Change in Likelihood to Purchase
Moving from $899 to $399	+54%	+44%
Moving from 4 inches to 8 inches	+9%	+16

Figure 6.1: Example of monitoring the change in preference share

The preference share tells us the likelihood that one package would be selected over another if the identified best/worst levels were the only changes made between the two bundles. The likelihood to purchase can only be determined if an alternative option is included in the exercise (none or dual choice). Using the simulator, we can calculate the likelihood that a $899 bundle would be selected versus purchasing nothing. We can then repeat that simulation with $399 and that will tell us the shift in likelihood to purchase when we move from the worst to the best level.

- What role does price play in decision making and what are the pricing sweet spots?

Pricing is a critical question that must be answered as part of product management and launching a product. What should you charge? Companies don't want to leave money on the table but also have legitimate concerns about pricing too high. Getting the price right can be the difference between a success and a flop. Conjoint is considered one of the best methodologies for tackling pricing questions. We can use the principles laid out in the previous questions to define the importance and impact of the price feature. If moving from the highest price (least favorable) to the lowest price (most favorable) causes a larger shift in selection behavior than changing any of the other features, it is the most influential feature. In the case that price is the most impactful feature, customers are paying a lot of attention to the price of the package when making their selection. In many conjoint analysis projects, price is the most important feature (as one might expect). On top of the influence that the overall price category has on preference and likelihood to purchase, conjoint can also shed light on price elasticity.

The most insightful approach for measuring price elasticity is to compare the same bundle vs the 'none' option while only changing the price of the bundle. The decrease in the simulator preference share as price is increased represents the relative demand. The exact preference share isn't as important as the size of the difference when changes are made. Below is an example of this using a conjoint project on yogurt where four price points were tested ($0.89, $1.19, $1.49, $1.79).

Simulator 1	None Option
Greek Yogurt	I would not purchase this yogurt
Mixed Berry	
6 oz	
Store brand	
$0.89	
72%	**28%**

Simulator 2	None Option
Greek Yogurt	I would not purchase this yogurt
Mixed Berry	
6 oz	
Store brand	
$1.19	
54%	**46%**

Simulator 3	None Option
Greek Yogurt	I would not purchase this yogurt
Mixed Berry	
6 oz	
Store brand	
$1.49	
51%	49%

Simulator 4	None Option
Greek Yogurt	I would not purchase this yogurt
Mixed Berry	
6 oz	
Store brand	
$1.79	
34%	66%

Figure 6.2: 4 screenshots from simulations ran where the package is held constant and only the price is altered.

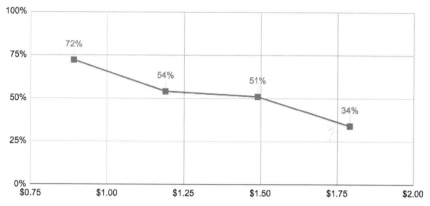

Price Elasticity vs None option

Figure 6.3: Here we can see that customers are much more sensitive moving from $0.89 to $1.19 and from $1.49 to $1.79 but the change is very minimal from $1.19 to $1.49. In a chart like this it is important to look at the slope of the lines as well as the inflection points or 'price elbows'.

- How sensitive will customers be to shifts in pricing?

  An argument for when you would want to include the none option or utilize dual-choice (also called dual-response) conjoint is because it allows one to measure the relative preference of the outside good. What is meant by 'outside good' is the respondent would either purchase another option (the competition) or purchase nothing at all. This is critically important for product and pricing teams as they can identify drop-off rates as variables are changed and price is increased. By comparing a bundle versus the option of not purchasing, we can glean insights into customer's sensitivity to price and pinpointing where revenue can likely be maximized.

- What is the monetary or relative value to the market of each of the features we are thinking about including? How much more would they be willing to pay for a premium feature?

Not only does conjoint analysis respond to questions about the total price of a package, it can also support the understanding of how much the individual components of the package are worth to a customer. This is very beneficial to companies because it helps them: back into what they should charge for the whole, better understand potential product margins and get a sense for what customers view as premium attributes. The metric that allows researchers to compartmentalize each element of the package and determine their value is Willingness to Pay. It is calculated by finding the amount of utility difference between the tested price points and then applying that dollar per utility ratio to the other levels and their utility scores. It can be used to compare how much monetary value the market places on one attribute versus another.

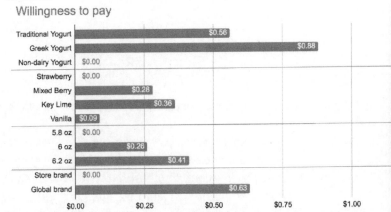

Figure 6.4: This chart showcases how much more the customer would pay for a yogurt attribute over the worst level of that feature group.

- What trade-offs will our customers be likely to make? If we know we need to increase price, what features/functionality can we add to our offering to not lose appeal and market share?

A common theme of conjoint analysis is 'trade-offs'; the idea being to gauge what customers are willing to give up in order to get. It is often the case where it would not make business-sense to include all of the top attributes that were included in the conjoint analysis exercise. There could be a multitude of reasons why companies can't do this, including: two attributes that are completely impossible to combine, not all features cost the same and maxing out each one could never produce returns, or combining levels would not be conducive to branding. This forces the business to decipher which trade-offs will yield the best results. Oftentimes, the trade-off in question is if increasing the price can be offset by adding in improved functionality. Conjoint is the perfect technique to understand this choice behavior because it produces a preference model for each individual that can be aggregated to simulate market behavior. If an individual has more positive utility for the superior feature than negative utility for the highest price, it makes sense to them to get the top feature even at the highest price.

Here is an example of how this can be brought to life using a simulator. We will keep all levels consistent and move the number of streamed movies available to the top level we tested accompanied by the highest price in one package. In the other we will incorporate the fewest number of movies and the lowest price.

	Option 1	Option 2	Add ⊕
Number of movies available	10	750	
Number of users	5	3	
Recommended movies	Yes	Yes	
Includes documentaries	No	No	
Price (per month)	$5.00	$25.00	
	41%	59%	

Figure 6.5: The simulator shows that customers are willing to trade-off paying more per month if they can get a lot more video titles available to them.

- *What does market share look like for different potential product bundles we are looking at? How does the altering of the bundle configuration affect market share?*

  This question specifically relies heavily on the simulator in its response. One note of caution is that conjoint analysis nor the simulator will predict exactly what market share a product configuration will obtain. It will provide guidance on the range a set of packages might fall within as well as the likelihood that each package would be selected when customers are presented with a lineup. Many researchers connect the likelihood that a bundle is selected/purchased to the share that it would garner in the market. This is most true if all of the options that a customer would have to choose from are available to be simulated.

  But to answer the question, conjoint analysis can yield insights into the shifts that happen in share of preference as other options are introduced. These options can be: not purchasing anything, can be a competitor's offering or could be another internal option where there are concerns of cannibalization. This would be done through setting lineups within a simulator and measuring the size of the shifts in likelihood to purchase as changes are made to the lineups.

- How do the product bundles we are considering compare to the competition? What can we do to best compete against what is currently on the market?

  Conjoint analysis can be a valuable tool in assessing how a potential product offering will fare against what is currently available on the market. This produces guidance toward how product configurations stack up to the competition and what gives the product the best chance at success. Additionally, it can point the researcher to where change in share is being pulled from, whether from the competition, the 'would not purchase' option or from their own existing product set.

A project where measuring up against the competition is part of the studies objectives, it is critical that the competition's product configurations are part of the variables being tested. If you don't test it, you can't simulate it. These can be included as either fixed options (similar to a none option) or to have their 'levels' be included with the rest of the levels being observed. With responses in hand and the modeling complete, the simulator should be used with the competitors and their bundle configurations covered as columns.

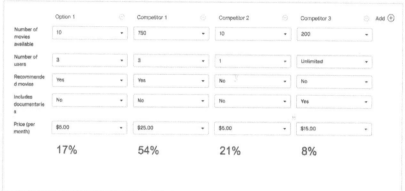

Figure 6.6: Showing how a potential bundle performs against the competitors in a simulator.

- *If we are looking to make changes to our existing product, what are the best improvements we can make? What will resonate best with our existing customers?*

To understand where there is room for improvement, businesses can use conjoint analysis to uncover where there is opportunity for the bettering of their product. With the output of conjoint, researchers can decipher the relative preference difference between the attributes tested. By observing which level within each feature has more utility than the current level of the product, the company can identify if potential changes are worth it. If organizations wish to explicitly observe the feelings and preferences of existing customers, the study should include sufficient sample of this demographic.

- What is the optimal product that we can offer to increase the number of buyers? To maximize our revenue? To maximize our profits?

These questions can actually have different answers and all can contribute to empowering product owners in their decision-making. The simulator is most likely the best tool in answering all of them.

There are distinct use cases where strategists have determined the most critical goal in launching a product is to maximize the number of buyers. They are interested in getting people in the door with the plan to win them over with product effectiveness and support that will motivate them to upgrade. In this case, they would want to minimize the 'non-purchasers' and build an option or lineup of options that connects with as many customers as possible. With the simulator, the researcher would want the none column to be as close to zero as possible. If this is an important question to answer, it would be essential to include a none option as part of the conjoint survey experience.

In order to understand how to maximize revenue, a company would also be interested in minimizing non-buyers but more importantly understand how much revenue those that are buying will generate. An example is if an organization charges $5 for their streaming service and expects 80% of potential customers to buy or if they charge $15 and 40% would sign up; which one is better? Simple math would tell us if we have 100 people 'in the market' and 80% would buy at $5, our revenue would be $400. But 40% at $15 would produce $600 and thus more revenue. Within the simulator, the researcher would want to set up a calculation that totals the amount of revenue produced from the lineup of packages by multiplying cost charged by the number of buyers (the preference share). There are optimization algorithms that can be used to find where revenue is maximized or a brute-

force approach can be used while running favorable packages in the simulator.

The next iteration on that would be to incorporate what the product configurations would cost the business so that margins and net profit can be calculated. With some products and services there is no additional cost of offering one level versus another and so optimization might look very similar to maximizing revenue. But in other cases, there can be significant differences such as switching from website FAQ support to email support to 24/7 phone support. In this case, the key metric of focus will be the net profit rather than revenue. Using a simulator, the researcher can know the profit of each package by multiplying the cost charged by the number of buyers and subtracting the cost for them to offer. Usually this is done by knowing the cost of each attribute being tested in the conjoint exercise and tabulating those being included in the bundle.

VII

Chapter 7: Business Examples of Conjoint Analysis

For this next chapter, we will consider different business experiences that would benefit from the insights obtained from conjoint analysis. Each example will focus on a made-up amusement park, **FunLand**, which has been around for 50 years but attendance and revenue have been slipping over the past couple of years. They have less customers showing up at the park. Customers that do show up aren't having a good experience and are not likely to visit the park again. FunLand isn't sure if it is their rides and amusements that are causing these unsatisfactory trips to the park or if it is the service they are receiving. Or maybe it is both? Word of these poor experiences is getting out and hurting their brand. Lastly, their employees are not happy. It is obvious that they are unengaged and uninterested and they know this is affecting the customer experience.

FunLand has some crucial questions they need to answer as changes must be made to stay relevant. They feel the opportunity is there but they will need to reinvent themselves in order to capture it but they will need to make changes quickly before it is too late.

Improving the Product Experience

FunLand's product is their park. It is the rides, the games, the entertainment and the food. It is everything that a customer interacts with on their grounds. FunLand added one new roller coaster ride last year but didn't see much of an uptick in purchased tickets. The rest of the park has remained relatively constant for the last decade. Adding that new ride was really expensive and didn't return the investment like they expected. FunLand isn't sure they have the time and funds to install another large attraction and so they are looking at other options; options that can provide major league results for minor league costs. If they are going to make changes to their product, they need to be confident it will move the needle.

The owner of FunLand recently attended a sporting event where the fans at the restaurants and bars in the concourse were having a better time than those sitting and watching the game. She thought about the boring burgers, fries, funnel cakes and corndogs that made up the food menu at FunLand. Maybe improving the food could be their route to improving their product? She was confident that it would be cheaper and quicker than opening a new ride.

Problem: FunLand has to improve what they offer to customers or they will go out of business.

Objective: Find an effective upgrade to their park that can be implemented quickly.

Hypothesis: FunLand can increase excitement about their product and retain customers by offering better food and beverage options. They will run a conjoint analysis study to understand what food alternatives provide the most excitement and lift.

They initiate the conjoint analysis by defining the features and levels that will represent the food possibilities available to customers. Here is what they are thinking:

1. Food Genres:
    a. Korean BBQ
    b. Thai
    c. Tex Mex
    d. Sushi
    e. Peruvian
    f. Hamburgers, Hotdogs, Corndogs (*currently offer*)
    g. Pizza (*currently offer*)
2. Restaurant Types:
    a. Fast Casual
    b. Buffet
    c. Food Truck
    d. Traditional Carnival Stands
3. Drink:
    a. Single Soda

        b. Unlimited Refillable Soda
        c. Single Beer
        d. Single Cocktail
    4. Food Speed:
        a. Less than 1 minute
        b. Less than 5 minutes
        c. 5 to 15 minutes
    5. Plate Cost Range:
        a. $5 to $10
        b. $10 to $20
        c. $15 to $30
        d. $20 to $40

They will also incorporate the incumbent options within the conjoint exercise. This will allow them to compare the potential lift against an existing benchmark. The researchers wanted to be really comprehensive with the included levels because they did not want to leave out a potential game-changing menu option.

Because of how opinionated people can be about food options, FunLand will move forward with an adaptive choice-based conjoint exercise. This will allow respondents to eliminate certain recipes that don't mesh with their taste buds and that would certainly heavily skew their survey selections.

Flow of the Survey:
- Screener questions
- Recreation and family activities questions
- Food and restaurant questions
- **Adaptive Conjoint Exercise**
    - Eliminate unacceptable food levels
    - Set of choice-based conjoint tasks
    - Likelihood to purchase winning concepts
- Demographics

(1/9) Which food option at FunLand is most appealing to you?

	Option 1	Option 2	None
Food Genre	Thai	Thai	
Restaurant Types	Traditional Carnival Stands	Buffet	I wouldn't buy food at
Drink	Unlimited Refillable Soda	Single Soda	FunLand if these were the
Food Speed	Less than 5 minutes	Less than 1 minute	options.
Plate Cost	$15 to $30	$15 to $30	
	○	○	○

Figure 7.1: Example of what the choice-based conjoint task looked like to respondents.

After programming the survey, they distributed it to both previous customers that they had email addresses for as well as a general Southern California population sample list. This allowed them to obtain a mixed sample.

The data came in and FunLand jumped right into the results. Initially they look at the core summary metrics.

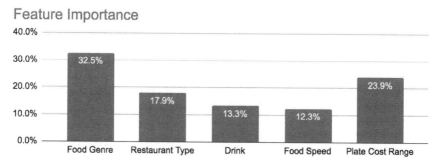

Feature Importance

40.0%
30.0% — 32.5%
20.0% — 23.9%
17.9%
10.0% — 13.3% — 12.3%
0.0%
Food Genre | Restaurant Type | Drink | Food Speed | Plate Cost Range

Figure 7.2: Feature Importance chart showcasing the percentage of range from moving from the worst level to the best level.

It is clear that the *food genre* is strongly impacting the concession selection as we would have suspected. It is even more important than how expensive the food is. We can further validate this with the simulator but the initial read says that we can charge more if we can deliver the right genres. Additionally, we see the preference for the different food speed levels to not be as impactful as the genre feature and might dictate that faster isn't better and quality is critical (better food traditionally takes longer to prepare).

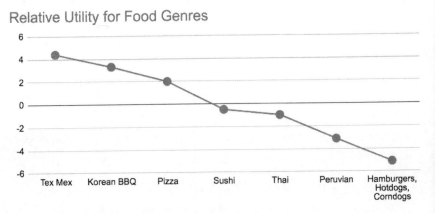

Relative Utility for Food Genres

Figure 7.3: View of the relationship between the different genres of food for initial relative comparisons.

Currently FunLand only offers the traditional hamburgers, hotdogs and corndogs as well as pizza. As we review the relative utility that is taken from the individual preference coefficients derived from the Bayesian model, we see that one of their main offerings is the least preferred option that we tested. Every other option should be able to produce a lift in interest and appeal and it looks like Tex Mex and Korean BBQ rise to the top. We will use this directionally as we move into the simulator and begin gauging how potential bundles perform.

Now FunLand turns their attention to the simulator. The first simulation will help them determine which lineup of three food genres (keeping the other features consistent) gives them the highest likelihood that someone would choose to eat at FunLand versus not eating.

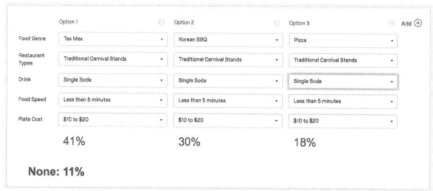

Figure 7.4: WIth the simulator in addition to using the relative utility chart of the preferences for the food genres as a head start, they tested several different bundles to identify where the 'None' option (not purchasing food) is minimized.

Next, they will use the simulator to determine if we offer the most preferred food offering for the highest price we tested and our current offering at the lowest price they tested, how does the preference share shake out? From this simulation, they see that customers are willing to pay more to get a great food experience.

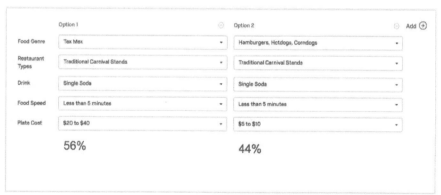

Figure 7.5: FunLand sees that the strength of offering the most appealing food genre (Tex Mex) is real. Even when they charge the highest price range, it still is more likely to be purchased than their current offering.

Lastly, the simulator reports that if we can nail the food options with quality and variety, we can increase attendees purchasing food increasing from 27% to 91%.

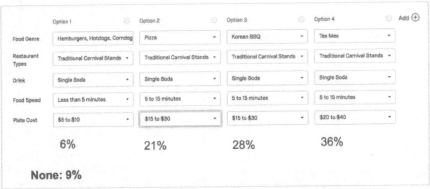

Figure 7.6: FunLand sees that their current option isn't highly likely of being purchased.

	Option 1	Option 2	Option 3	Option 4	Add ⊕
Food Genre	Hamburgers, Hotdogs, Corndogs	Pizza	Korean BBQ	Tex Mex	
Restaurant Types	Traditional Carnival Stands	Traditional Carnival Stands	Traditional Carnival Stands	Traditional Carnival Stands	
Drink	Single Soda	Single Soda	Single Soda	Single Soda	
Food Speed	Less than 5 minutes	5 to 15 minutes	5 to 15 minutes	5 to 15 minutes	
Plate Cost	$5 to $10	$15 to $30	$15 to $30	$20 to $40	
	6%	21%	28%	36%	

None: 9%

Figure 7.6: A new lineup significantly reduces the likelihood of not purchasing and gets some new exciting options for the customers.

Improving the Brand Experience

FunLand is trying to gauge the value of their brand in comparison to the other amusement park options of Southern California. They want to know the community's perception of FunLand and the role the brand plays when making their purchase decision for entertainment. They knew they had brand issues of being out-of-touch and old but before they could address it, they wanted to better understand the relative value of their brand versus the competition. This insight could provide direction to who has the best brand and how much more could one brand charge then the others if all else was equal.

Problem: FunLand's is struggling to ascertain exactly what their brand is and what it is worth.

Objective: Find the value of their brand and how it compares to the competition.

Hypothesis: FunLand will have less brand preference than the competition but knowing the value will help dictate if price of entry changes need to be made.

Here are the conjoint attributes that will be included in this brand-focused conjoint study:

1. Brand:
   a. FunLand
   b. Disneyland
   c. Knott's Berry Farm
   d. Six Flags
   e. SeaWorld
   f. Legoland
2. Ride wait times:
   a. 10min
   b. 15min
   c. 30min
   d. 1 hour
3. Business hours:
   a. 9am to 5pm
   b. 8am to 8pm
   c. 6am to 11pm
4. Price of entry:
   a. $25 per day
   b. $50 per day
   c. $75 per day
   d. $100 per day
   e. $150 per day
   f. $200 per day

(1/8) Choose the option below you would be most likely to purchase.

	Option 1	Option 2	None
Brand	FunLand	Legoland	I wouldn't choose either of these options
Ride wait times	10min	1 hour	
Business hours	8am to 8pm	8am to 8pm	
Price of entry	$150 per day	$75 per day	
	◉	◉	◉

Figure 7.7: Example of a conjoint task in this study

FunLand deployed the conjoint survey to both the local population of Southern California as well as a sample of respondents from the continental United States. They want to understand the perception of the differences in the two groups.

The first step for FunLand was to see how much brand played in decision-making of respondents in comparison to the other features tested, especially price. We gauge this with the feature importance score.

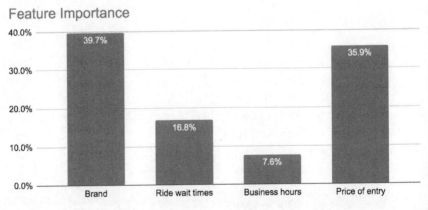

Figure 7.8: Glimpse at the importance of the different features

Not surprisingly, *Brand* and *Price of entry* were by far the biggest players in how customers decide what park to attend. And piecing together this feature importance insight with the chart below of the preference share (likelihood of being the observed or selected choice) of the different individual brands, we know we have an uphill battle. We knew with everything being equal, that Disneyland was going to be the leader. They have a much stronger brand. But there is power in knowing and now we can plan a strategy around improving our brand, tailoring our offering and developing our pricing strategy.

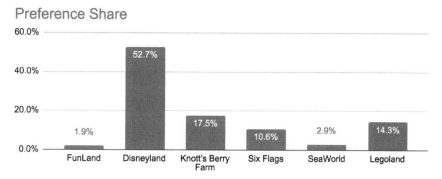

Figure 7.9: Shows the likelihood of each brand being selected when all else is equal

Below is a look at the relative dollar value (can be interpreted as willingness to pay) of each of the brands in comparison to FunLand that is derived from the delta in the cost over the delta in the utility.

Figure 7.10: Shows the relative utility value of price of entry for the willingness to pay calculation

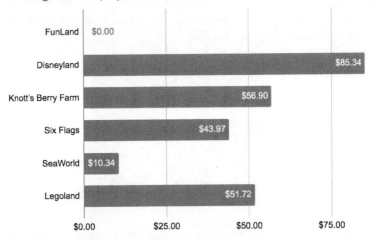

Willingness to pay vs FunLand

FunLand	$0.00
Disneyland	$85.34
Knott's Berry Farm	$56.90
Six Flags	$43.97
SeaWorld	$10.34
Legoland	$51.72

$0.00 $25.00 $50.00 $75.00

Figure 7.11: Willingness to pay metric for each of the brands in comparison to FunLand

From this they can interpret that customers would pay $85 more to attend Disneyland than FunLand. Their brand is worth significantly more. This is how conjoint analysis can be extremely insightful for informing researchers on the relative value of a brand and how it can be measured in purchase decisions.

Improving the Employee Experience

FunLand knows that a major problem they face is a disengaged workforce that certainly is not going the extra mile to deliver a great customer experience. Unfortunately, they have countless emails about disinterested and uncaring staff members. They have done their research and know that happy employees result in happy customers. There is also extremely high turnover within their employee base with employees quickly jumping ship. So, part of the full force attack in trying to reinvent FunLand is addressing the employee issue.

FunLand realizes that in order to combat this, they will need to invest back into their employees and their experience in order to spark a change. But there will need to be limits with how much can be put back towards the workforce so FunLand needs to identify where they can produce the most bang for the buck. They must understand what employees are willing to give up in order to get and how they can make the most of every dollar they invest.

The idea has come to them to use a conjoint analysis study to understand these employee trade-offs and gauge what can yield the most utility to better inspire their team.

Problem: FunLand's employees are not engaged and not delivering a great customer experience .
Objective: Find what benefits can be offered that will excite employees, keep them around and motivate them to provide a better experience to customers.
Hypothesis: Certain benefits such as giving back to employees in terms of their education will be really preferred and can be used as incentives for them to be more engaged at work.

Here are the conjoint attributes that will be included in this employee benefits conjoint study:

1. Education reimbursement (if employee stays a year)
    a. No reimbursement
    b. $1,000 per year
    c. $3,000 per year
    d. $5,000 per year
2. Paid Time Off
    a. No paid time off
    b. 1 day per month
    c. 10 days to be used any time over the year
3. Perks
    a. 1 free meal per 8-hour shift
    b. Unlimited fountain drinks while working
    c. 1 free family pass per week
    d. Unlimited park access when not working
4. Salary
    a. $10 per hour with $5 raise every subsequent year
    b. $12.50 per hour with $2.50 raise every subsequent year
    c. $15 per hour

d. $17.50 per hour
5. Bonus
   a. $250 bonus after 2 months
   b. $500 bonus after 5 months
   c. $1,000 bonus after 1 year
   d. $250 bonus for each month as a top performer

(1/8) Choose the employee benefit package below you prefer most:

	Package 1	Package 2
Education reimbursement	No reimbursement	$3,000 reimbursement per year
Paid Time Off	1 day per month	10 days to be used any time over the year
Perks	Unlimited fountain drinks while working	1 free meal per 8 hour shift
Salary	$10 per hour with $2 raise every subsequent year	$16 per hour
Bonus	$250 bonus after 2 months	$500 bonus after 5 months
	◉	◉

Figure 7.12: Conjoint task for understanding the employee experience

The conjoint survey was then sent to FunLand employees to get their honest assessment of various benefit offerings.

They immediately looked at where employees were placing their focus at the category level. Specifically, they wanted to see how important *'Education reimbursement'* was in comparison to the other categories.

Feature Importance

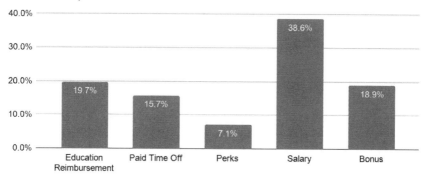

Figure 7.13: Glimpse at the importance of the different features

Salary drew the most focused of the benefit package but the Education Reimbursement is something that employees are paying significant attention to and it looks like the hypothesis is correct. Subsequently, FunLand is going to test the trade-offs of the workforce with complete bundles.

Using the simulator, FunLand first examines what they can configure to help offset the importance employees are placing on Salary. They want to be really careful with Salary because it has significant P&L impact and is a one-way door.

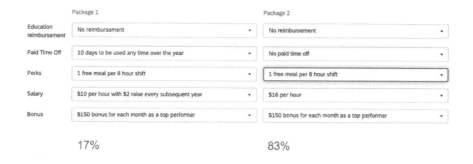

Figure 7.14: Simulation of 10 PTO days and $10/hour salary vs no PTO and $16/hour salary

They see that sticking to the current salary ($10 per hour) has a significant impact on the appeal of the benefits package as it has a very small preference share and is not liked.

	Package 1		Package 2	
Education reimbursement	$5,000 reimbursement per year	▾	No reimbursement	▾
Paid Time Off	10 days to be used any time over the year	▾	No paid time off	▾
Perks	1 free meal per 8 hour shift	▾	1 free meal per 8 hour shift	▾
Salary	$10 per hour with $2 raise every subsequent year	▾	$16 per hour	▾
Bonus	$500 bonus after 5 months	▾	$150 bonus for each month as a top performer	▾

66%   44%

Figure 7.15: Including $5,000 tuition reimbursement to the simulation in Figure 7.14

FunLand identifies that if they can really pump resources towards Education, Paid Time Off and Bonus, it can be an even more preferred trade-off than the current benefits package with the inclusion of a higher salary. They were correct in their thinking that there is a lot of potential with Education Reimbursement with their young workforce.

Improving the Customer Experience

FunLand wants to be known for delivering an incredible customer experience but right now that is not the case. As part of the customer interviews that have been conducted, a frequently mentioned frustration has been the wait times while waiting to ride. An easy solve would be to increase the number of rides and attractions at FunLand. But unfortunately, the resources to make that happen are prohibitive. They need to find a more scrappy approach rather than add another multimillion-dollar attraction. What can they incorporate in the lines to reduce the frustration?

Problem: FunLand is not delivering a great customer experience and a big factor is the wait times for the rides. They will not be able to add more attractions though to further disburse riders.

Objective: Find experiences and entertainment that can be introduced as part of the long lines for the rides.

Hypothesis: That if FunLand adds the right experiences to the line, we can reduce the annoyance that customers are currently complaining about.

Here are the conjoint attributes that will be included in this customer experience conjoint study:

1. Wait time
   a. 15 minutes
   b. 30 minutes
   c. 1 hour
   d. 1.5 hours
2. Experience
   a. Food and drink samples
   b. Arcade games
   c. High speed WIFI
   d. None
3. Entertainment
   a. TV's showing sports, news and music videos
   b. Song and dance live performers
   c. Meet and greet mascots and characters

As part of this conjoint study it will be important to include a 'None' option as it represents a customer avoiding the line altogether. This will be key in serving as a baseline and in answering the question of 'is this line experience appealing enough for customers to wait?'.

(1/4) Imagine you were at a theme park and you had the following options for 2 different rides that you were interested in. **Select the line you would be more likely to wait in**. If you wouldn't wait in either line, please select the 'None' option.

	Ride 1	Ride 2	None
Wait Time	1 hour	15 minutes	
Experience	Arcade games	Arcade games	I would not wait in either of these lines.
Entertainment	TV's showing sports, news and music videos	Meet and greet mascots and characters	
	⊙	⊙	⊙

Figure 7.16: Conjoint task for understanding the customer experience

The survey was sent to the general population as well as those in a customer database to get a further read on those familiar with the rides at FunLand.

The analyst first wanted to do some checks to ensure people understood the conjoint exercise. They did this by examining the relative preference for the line wait times. This matches what they would have expected; longer wait times equals less preference.

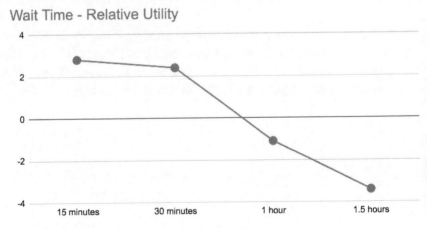

Figure 7.17: Charting the relative utility of wait times

Next, they wanted to measure the likelihood of someone choosing an average package at the different wait times versus avoiding the line altogether (none option). The chart below checks out that respondents properly understood the exercise as we see the expected ride selection likelihood seriously drop as wait time increases.

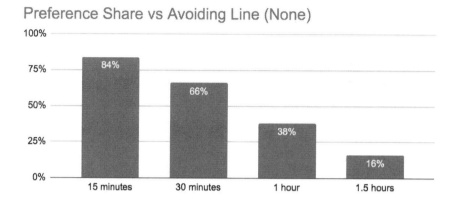

Figure 7.18: Showcasing the likelihood that someone would stay in line (all else remaining equal) as wait time increases

In furthering their analysis, FunLand wants to see how much the wait time impacted decisions in comparison to the *Experience* and *Entertainment* features. To no surprise *Wait Time* factored in more than the other feature in the decisions the respondents were making.

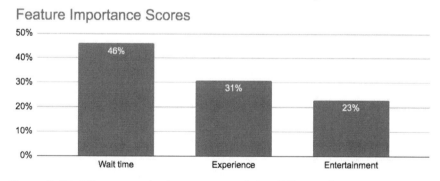

Figure 7.19: Glimpse at the importance of the different features

There is opportunity however with the right combination of *Experience* and *Entertainment* to offset longer times. FunLand wants to further look into those combinations to see where customers skipping rides can be minimized. They crank up the simulator to identify what can be done.

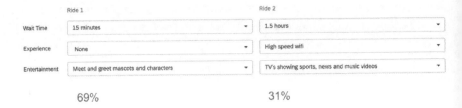

69%   31%

Figure 7.20: Simulating packaging including short wait time vs long wait times

Initially they look at if providing high speed internet to those in lines would make up for long wait times. The simulator clearly shows that isn't enough. But what if they can provide food samples and drinks? They like this idea because it can also introduce patrons to new food/drink options. They look to the simulator to understand what that can offer.

53%   47%

Figure 7.21: Simulating what can be done to offset long wait times

It doesn't become more favorable to the 15-minute wait time option but it does get pretty close which is a win in FunLand's book.

Next they look at how this option would fare against skipping the lines altogether.

	Ride 1
Wait Time	1.5 hours
Experience	Food and drink samples
Entertainment	TV's showing sports, news and music videos

59%

None: 41%

Figure 7.22: Simulating what the improved package would look like vs avoiding the line altogether (None)

FunLand is really excited about this option because a 1.5 hour wait with no 'experience' had a 7% likelihood to be selected (preference share) vs no line at all. Without the ability to really shorten lines by adding new attractions, FunLand decides to start treating the customers with hors d'oeuvres as they await the roller coaster.

VIII

Chapter 8: Recap of Conjoint Analysis

The goal of this book was to introduce and detail the powerful research tool that conjoint analysis is. It can be an extremely useful and flexible approach at understanding how products and services can best be assembled. In the previous section we went through a number of use cases of conjoint analysis for a made-up business. However, conjoint extends well beyond just these cases and is relatively limitless in regard to the different business objectives it can shed light on.

To reiterate, conjoint analysis is a research methodology that measures the preferences that customers have for the different elements that could potentially make up a product. It captures the trade-offs likely to be made by the market by presenting survey takers with a set of different bundles and observing which ones they like most. Based upon those choices, models can be prepared to predict the performance of any given bundle. This statistical modeling is what can make conjoint daunting and complex but also makes it accurate, insightful and actionable.

When I first came to Qualtrics, there were just a couple of us. Everyone wore *a lot* of hats. As one of the only employees with a math background, I got assigned to assist a customer who had requested help in running their conjoint analysis project. The problem was, I didn't know what conjoint was. Luckily, one of our founders, Scott Smith, was a renowned market research professor with decades of experience with conjoint analysis. He mentored me and taught me the principles. I immediately was enamored with conjoint as it was a perfect blend of marketing and math. I recognized its reach and value. These were the projects I wanted to be working on and I spent the next decade working with customers on their studies as well as doing as much research as I could on this topic. Projects came in from every type of business and from all over the world. From helping a global technology company redesign their support offering with the goal of increasing preference while reducing the users tendency to want to call in. Or a nationally-ranked college football team looking to make changes to their stadium experience. Or working with a prestigious financial services organization to improve their employee benefits package to combat above expected attrition. There have been loads of studies that we have been able to participate in. It was a great privilege to take part in all of this research and to use conjoint analysis to provide critical insights.

Conjoint analysis is an ever-evolving science that has been morphing since its initiation. Advancements in conjoint has further tailored the respondent experience, improved the predictive modeling of the output and taken advantage of improvements in technology. As software continues to move forward, conjoint analysis is becoming more and more of a research technique that can be utilized by anyone. Conjoint is being simplified in a way that reduces the intimidation that accompanies conjoint analysis historically. There is incredible potential with conjoint analysis to both (1) create and develop new conjoint approaches and (2) tackle new types of projects and studies with this research method. And so that is my challenge to the reader: to think of business problems to be tackled and how conjoint analysis can be applied in new and creative ways in order to understand the decision behavior of your audience.

About the Author

Craig Lutz has been a data scientist and researcher at Qualtrics since 2007. He has presented at conferences on the subject of quantitative research methods and has conducted thousands of conjoint analysis projects for Qualtrics' customers over his time there. He also designed and developed Qualtrics' conjoint analysis DIY technology that empowers users to conduct their own studies.

Craig graduated from BYU with a degree in Actuarial Science. He serves as the Executive Chairman of Ball Is Life. Craig and his wife Karrie have 4 kids and reside in Orem, Utah.

Printed in Great Britain
by Amazon

29969655R00044